ordinary chaos

ordinary chaos

kimberly kruge

Carnegie Mellon University Press
Pittsburgh 2019

ACKNOWLEDGMENTS

Grateful acknowledgment is made to the kind editors of the following journals in which these poems appeared:

Bloodroot: "Enumeration at the Immigration Office" and "Canto for Two Women Who Commissioned a Love Poem"; *The Collagist*: "Love Poem for the Purported End of the World"; *The Denver Quarterly*: "Radio María"; *The Iowa Review*: "Panther in the Primavera" and "A Phenomenalist's Guide to the Block"; *The Massachusetts Review*: "Pilgrimage"; *Omniverse*: "Direct Address"; *Ploughshares*: "If, Then"; *Poetry Northwest*: "Apology"; *Puerto del Sol*: "After the Election"; *Precog*: "Walk" (and its Spanish translation); *RHINO*: "Live from the U.S."; *Spoon River Poetry Review*: "Potable Water Anecdote" and "La Bestia"; *Tinderbox Poetry Journal*: "The Morning Newspaper"; *Twyckenham Notes*: "María"; *Witness*: "Articulation" (excerpts)

Special thanks to the Center for Book Arts for publishing a limited edition of a chapbook entitled *High-Land Sub-Tropic*, in which twenty pages of poetry from this collection also appear. *High-Land Sub-Tropic* was selected as the winner of the 2017 Center for Book Arts Chapbook Prize by Juan Felipe Herrera. The following poems from this manuscript also appear in the chapbook: "Apology," "Loosed Sestina," "Current," "Radio María," "If, Then," "Marriage," "Bread Man," "Se Busca," "Walk," "El 24," "A Phenomenalist's Guide to the Block," "Patria," "Panther in the Primavera," "Celebration," "River of Waste/River of Stones," and "Pilgrimage." This same chapbook is available in a bilingual edition published in Mexico.

"The Wall" and "True" were part of a feature on the Negative Capability Press site.

I would also like to thank those who have been my wise mentors, careful readers and steadfast supporters, especially:

Heather McHugh, Cleopatra Mathis, Martha Rhodes, Stephen Dobyns, Connie Voisine, Bruce Coffin, Rick Barot, Gabrielle Calvocoressi, Jennifer Hart, Taryn Tilton, Tessa Murphy, Carrie Mar, Jennifer Büchi, Claudia Rángel, Jennifer Funk, Laura Swearingen-Steadwell, Kaisa Edy, Geoff Kronik, Rolf Yngve, Nathan McClain, The Kruge Family, Fiona Lundie and Family, Julie Delphin and Family, Gabriela Collins-Fernández and Family, Alexis López and Family

Book design by Juliana Schnerr

for Alexis

CONTENTS

I. CHASM

II. EXOSKELETON

III. NEGATIVE SPACE

I: CHASM

RADIO MARÍA

There was a break in the housenumbers on Calle San Juan Bosco that year,
the year in which I didn't know how to communicate but with my hands.
The taxi driver and I, lost, looking for the badnumber that marked a subtracted
space between a pigeon flock and an old money house—somewhere in the middle,
Radio María's mast had not been figured out of the street's badmath. The Virgin in her habit
on the station's sign. AM 920. Guadalajara. We could always ask the nuns for help.
If I could only ask. The taxi driver and I, there, with our deadwords. Music. *Do you like.*
I do like. The taxi driver throws up his hands and goes. Alone: Radio María minus pigeon flock
plus old money house equals key left for me to the badnumber apartment where I will
live for years and the neighbor will die and the newcomer will drunk drive his car into the sidewall
and the tree will receive lightning and the pigeons will tear the street straight up from the world
when they take off. But the building will never fall. The blankdoor will never be painted any other
way but blank. And, Radio María.

Radio María sends her signal out to the city. Radio María sends her signal out to the ocean
I believed was at the end of the city when I believed the city was a city made for the sea and
if only I took that street and not this one I would end up on the border of land and all the ocean's
timevoices. If I forget that the ocean is not really there, it will be there again. And Radio María
sending her voice against time. Radio María saving lost souls of maritime tragedies. Radio María
breaking high, breaking low. Radio María hymning to fisherman. Radio María casting a net
and coming up full of deadwords. Radio María listening to the amplitude modulation of my mind
though I've never listened to hers. Radio María knowing how it ends. Knowing how to end it.
Badmath: Radio María minus badnumber plus deadwords equals the key won't be left,
the neighbor will not die, the newcomer won't newcome, the wall falls, the tree falls,
the street has no place but the ground and sound does not a metaphor make. That year,
in which I didn't know how to communicate but with my hands, I still really knew something.

IF, THEN

If the men from town call in the crux of night,
then they are calling to misinform you.

If they say *come quick your brother's in jail,*
then that's not what they mean.

If you go to town but your brother's not in jail,
then this time he cannot be saved.

If your brother cannot be sprung from a cage,
then he couldn't have been saved anyways.

If the men from town call in the crux of night,
then it's not because of *that* but *this*:

death. If the men from town have to lie,
then they tell a nebulous lie. Detained's less direct than

dead. If you must think about the body,
then you cannot let it get to you. Remember:

if your brother or anyone's brother could've been saved
then he would've been saved but if,

if a man falls into the machine at the quarry,
then that machine gets full-mouthed with power &

if a man looks back up at life from the machine,
then he's still headed down to death. It's just that

if life's hand won't reach out into someplace,
then death's hand will & you,

if you cannot forget what you saw in the morgue,
then it's not your fault, it's death's—

   not too modest to put its hand on your back,
   tell you where the comfort's at, go:

   the mind is a rogue machine. If humane then inhumane.
       The nebulous night reaches in.

PANTHER IN THE PRIMAVERA

And then, my husband was alone in the woods with the panther. Not a real panther, of course, but the old wives' tale panther, with hand-spun fur and whittled teeth. With a romanticized grin and prettied-up paws. You see, Guadalajara was disappearing, and there was only one reserve left, the Primavera, and those who thought they knew the woods, those who thought that they were in a covert and sacred situation with the woods, let's call it, a conversation, wanted to remain part of it. Wanted to be preserved like a ring in the fog of its enduring morning. Those who didn't want enough to be part of it caught rumor of the panther and never went back. This was the test, let's call it, of faith. And one by one, all had their faith broken. One by one, my husband was left more and more alone in the woods. Now, I can only imagine my husband, using a voice he only uses around the woods, that he snaps up into his throat when he hears a rustle. Alone out there with fabled animals and their fabulous hungers. Alone out there with history laid out before him. Alone out there in front of a mirror of obsidian. Splitting peace like bread with the wild. Eyes upcast like those of a consecrated statue. The panther eating from his hand. His mind slightly agape. His ex-thoughts a whorl of petrified wood. My husband alone in the woods, in conversation, rooting. Cultivating an appendage I'll never know. Speaking in tongues. Maybe, even, performing miracles. I am not out to know but to turn my mind over like a leaf or stone.

13

RIVER OF WASTE/RIVER OF STONES

(The debated etymology of "Guadalajara")

that the tongue is negative capability

a skeleton building raises itself up against
the haze horizon—voices of the land in the spaces

between its bones the hills speaking from the grave in lost
etymology *River of Waste* and or *River of Stones*

the tongue works and unworks   the tongue catches
and doesn't catch   the tongue makes word and

makes space   light and dark   is
the industrious stone / the squandered source

BREAD MAN

It isn't simple like, if you can push one thing you can push another, or, if you can push one thing you can push anything. Some people are best at or like pushing one thing and one thing only: candy, bread, ice cream, drug, fruit, handiwork, suits, souls, maize, art. I, for example, only push words like from door to door in a broken cart at daytime. The blind man of the morning pushes peanut marzipan, the blind man of the afternoon laminated reproductions of Christ, the blind man of the night bright straw dolls with black loops for eyes. Another man, the half-blind man of all 24 hours, only pushes stories from his bucket stoop on the corner: Today he's got work for my husband pushing gelatines, yesterday he heard that tomorrow they are going to land a 737 alongside the temple, right down onto the shredded pavement of Calle Contreras Medellin. The computer of his mind pushes everything to him. Some people don't want for anything enough to push and the push comes to them. I don't say this like a bad thing. When I need someone to push something to me, say, push a clean glass of water or a clean window, I find no one.

Some tíos can push more than one thing. I know a tío—sweetest tío you'll ever meet—who knows how to push the process of bread, bigger than bread itself. He can push the aroma of the process of making a butter loaf right into the whetting glands of your mind. He can shape from just two hands and the air a chocolate creme-filled sweet loaf. Sweetest tío you'll ever meet. He'll pull your chair out for you and go to the corner, a far corner, just for the soda you like. He can push the regular loaf, wheat loaf, oat loaf, flaxseed loaf, muffins, rolls, even the little pastries they renamed Nitos from Negritos when the company got some half-baked conscience about pushing words. This tío can push the whole factory, the night shift, "Positivity" onto the "Negative" aire of a newcomer, the benefits of one's controlling one's own mind, the public transportation system, the street, the neighborhood, the love. The streets can come to fear a man like that. A man who can push bread and love of family alike but in the different, right ways. Versatile. Canny. Provident. It isn't simple like, if anyone pushes one thing they can or will push another anything. Not just anyone can push the night into the rain's end, into the first warm, gray streaks of morning—this morning, last morning, next morning—at a factory far on the outskirts pushing in, then push the bread out early to the block, to the corner, to you. The streets can come to revere a push like that.

SE BUSCA

A whole country tacking signs to trees
and riding its proverbial horses out

into what were once the woods
in search of fire or food—

whole towns named for the wood
which makes fire best: pine, oak, ash.

A whole country seeking its beloved,
tacking to trees *se busca* where

x is sought, x: the dog,
x: the child, x: the aunt—

the paper which makes fire best:
inquiry, lack, want.

What deficient heads we have,
that in this ardent want

or a conflagration of thought we lose
x: the accused or x: the person

who'd sought even once, us,
wrapping their legs around

the midsection of our lives,
dousing our need for loss.

For three years a girl named Rain's husband had been lost—
went out one day never to come back

and not in the way the discontent decide, but like this:
the man goes out a day like any to barter goods for gold,

out where a country is still country and trees still trees,
a fire still a fire, and a proverb strictly a proverb;

he loses his way and never finds it again.
Tell the children he never finds it again.

Rain never hears a whisper of what happened to that man
until now: *he was found in a well. Found dead in a well?*

I have to hear her say *dead. A well in Tamaulipas* says Rain.
Found dead in a well in Tamaulipas? But she says,

then my subconscious became encapsulated—
something only Rain can say. *In Tamaulipas,* meaning

place where many prayers are said, a word with two roots.
Tell me the whole story over from the beginning,

this time, not leaving out anything.
Yes, found dead. Of course, found dead.

A whole country tacking signs to trees
and hanging posters from bridges:

se busca the father, *se busca* the way
se busca the well, *se busca* the clearing.

Signs stay up even when x
is found and rain takes down

the vestige: seed for this country
that wants least to need. The nothing

which never disappears, the everything
which never finds its way home.

In the language of a country seeking x,
the root of *buscar* is contested.

No one can trace the word back.
No one can unearth it right.

˙CELEBRATION

                    see:
two men kissing in the street
    two weeks after it's legal

in front of the neighborhood temple
    and its little-known statues

two men kissing in the underwing
    sweep of streetlight wrapt

classical beauties reflected
    on the window of the art supply

a mother hurries her child by
    but the men are outside of time

a worker on his way home stops
    to watch and I watch

the worker watch the men
    but the men are outside of observation

police pass in their stealth black
    panther of a truck hungry for nothing

the worker stares down the canal of night
    into its mouth of darkness

waits for the bus that doesn't come
    to this corner ever   feigns

he's not their voyeur and actually
    he's not that but instead

heavy with longing for his life
    like pressing lips to the past's figure

in its red shirt   his hands on its back
    its sacred mantle   under the protective wing

of light on lesser-known streets
    let this moment of glory

be a reminder to us all
    bystanders in this triangulated renaissance

masterpiece, witnesses to this
    newly ordained miracle of liberty

on the corner of San Felipe & Contreras Medellin
    who were a missionary & a militant

the heavy stone bell tower has been
    singing all its life something else

    now: glory
glory   glory

AFTER A PARTY

having gone out there past
the military trucks of faces,
lost boys and the edge
of reality as we know it,

        where the city rounds,
        in fat arteries, a heavy rhythm—
        the sad, church step of an organ;
        having gone out there, where I couldn't
name a single plant in its sway,
there for the celebration of an unknown woman—
having drunk, having said thick lies,
having shaken hands and unsealed my pink mouth,

        having seen the thirty-something with her sunken face
        and weight on her eyes, celebrant, and her downward
        lips—she knew my name—how terrible—
        having gone out there, to those few small tables
in a vast place rented
for celebration, where two girls told red-
secrets into their cups (and I imagined
they loved each other)—

        having watched the invitees wade
        in their eyes, drunk on whitewater swigs,
        having heard them sing to themselves
        in the royal light of the jukebox,
(?) what does it matter now, when,
my husband, having killed a millepede
with his dress shoe against the bedroom wall,
swears not to let it leave a mark

        when, in this state, all I can think
        is what kind of glutted life was
        erupted so exuberantly on the wall
        and then:
the crushing sensation that
I'll never lose the memory of
tonight, solely for its being
unlike any other,

but that entire aspects of my husband,
the thousand centers of his apologies,
will be lost simply because he is consistent
and not too much for sentiment.

ESOTERICISM ON REFORMA

The future is being sold on the corner.

The women, the stoop mystics, hate my shoes.
They start their gaze up from my feet to my
calves then thighs as if figuring up from the
ground the hex they're going to put on me.
Maybe they've already done it. Maybe they've
laced a clear magic through the glass of me here
as I listen to my mother's voice through the long
unseeable connection across Place. Maybe they've
brought La Santa Muerte in on it, red-veiled like
a hint at history, she is: parturition, root and rot.
Maybe I'm a part of their indiscriminate order,
their stare that moves now up past my stomach
to the warm apple of my heart and the sad soft peach
of my chin. *When, for you, a child?* the oldest reads
with sun-bleached eyes. *After X?* She reads left to right.
Before Y? She reads top to bottom. *At point Z?*
She reads through me. The stoop mystics stare
through me from the corner of Reforma.

How here we name even the streets
for that which we think we should want.

EL 24

The stranger and I: two people going home in the middle of the day like people who've got nothing to do. We are the two luckiest souls in the whole of humanity, spread ten seats apart in the lightness of the near-vacant bus; we're bouncing on the bliss blue chairs of the carnival orange *El 24* as it barrels over the legal route, and then in an illegal turn of events, takes us down into the high-speed tunnels, public transportation's prohibited city. Not once does demise cross our minds. The stranger looks at me, her open, wild, mouth full of candy-white teeth, her eyes wide like two pert balloons. We're going home, we're going home, on this illicit express, the fast tile of the tunnel washing clean our minds. How many homes that aren't ours we've passed. How the day looks up there. How the TV station waves its red sadness. How short-haired María begs so good you don't know she's begging. How peculiarities are hustled: the stirrups, boots and belts store with parking for cowboys only; the ostrich products store with a cure for everything, the pregnancy corset place over by the civil registry, the megachurch in the defunct nightclub. The stranger and I could see all of it clear as yesterday in our minds if we wanted to, but right now we don't know how to, our minds clean like fruitless vines or unset tables with none of those olive shoots sitting up around them wanting. How all the kids cry up there and the ground-down heels tap in wait at the stops. How life happens or how time goes by.

Out of the tunnel, I do know, relatively, where my home is, but I don't know either, and that's no deep thought, just the reality of things. We're over by the bowling lanes and the immigrant monument and the streets named for stars, but the reality of things is I always get the constellations crossed and undo the map. The bus driver's eyes look straight ahead, and he calmly smokes an individually sold cigarette. Not once has demise crossed our minds, stranger, so, let's keep riding. I won't pull the cord if you don't, and we'll come to the ranches and then the lake and then all the dormant volcanoes and the live one, then to the Pacific. No one waits for people who ride the bus in the middle of the day like they've got nowhere to go. An extraordinary hand can be played on a runaway bus that just makes off with two people: two strangers on the notorious *24* which, every day but today, stumbles, a floundering brute, through time and light and its trajectory like a body ahead of its mind in the dark house it knows.

PATRIA

Boys washing windshields
in traffic on a Friday evening,
the post-rain streaked sun behind,
the pre-rain elephantine
cloud getting situated over
the city center—*it must now be*
raining on the fat alligator
skin of my limes and the hearty
wisp of wayward weeds
that clench the orange beak
of my bird of paradise—the boys'
studded jeans rubbing up
on the hoods of cars and
their crystal eyes in the gray
reflection of all this glass—
the rain must be right above
my roof now: juicy, heavy
drops flinging through
the century-old
brick ventilation
onto my specked and cracked
tile floor, must be watermarking
the leather of the couch like spit—
the windshield boys with
FM radios on their hips,
"banda" up full tilt, music like
a carnival of a lost place—
how the rain must be
really coming down now,
a hurl of undistinguishable
single sounds on the tin roof,
the wind scouring my curtains,
taking down another page
of my newsprint blinds—what
the politician did, the soccer star,
the diva did, the quarter-page
obituary, the headline *"Light and*
Time"—and these boys here with
sagging pockets, heavy with coins,

the smallest fractions
of national currency—no one I know
is too proud to use a handful
of the tiniest coins to pay for their
admission or need. Here at this
traffic stop, between where the rain
has been and where it goes,
under the wrought iron windows
of a neighborhood that used to
be bad but now is just a place
where you can find anything
or get lost on a side street,
the sun is coming down,
getting under the
rubber ball gone out of bounds,
the pots of food left out to lull,
the blankets of the bedridden,
getting under the
staidness, the silence, the stead-
fastness of what it means
to be alright with things. *All*—

just when I thought I didn't love my country.

MARRIAGE

Rings of rain in the
flood. I never want to be,
I know, without *this*.

•

Years. I still don't know
which light switch goes to which room.
Probability.

•

This: that you enjoy
the sore drip of the shower
on sober shoulders.

•

Fireworks go off
in midday luminescence.
We exchange no glance.

•

This: exuberance!
The day releases wild flocks
behind your mind's eye.

•

Any minute now
the sky'll come down to hold court
on the wash line, wet.

•

This: the night whimper:
the late mother of your dreams
opens her lost house.

•

A purple crest on
your eyelid encroaches. I
see death's first wave there.

•

This: the rounds of your
hands circle like a God's eye
of laced ancestries.

•

The gate to a not
before seen house reveals a
tenuous tangle.

•

Accumulations
of that which you don't discard.
This: your saneness swings.

•

Our home works alone.
We abandon, return, wait
in the half-open.

•

This: what you have not
observed. I hold images
for you. We change hands.

•

The garden lives. Dies.
Drowns. Flourishes. Drops ripe fruit.
It undoes unwant.

•

The iris of sex,
this diaphanous petal.
See: even silence.

•

Lightning strikes in the
patio. Or so we think—
our heads in bright sleep.

PILGRIMAGE

Egress: how does it work with the Virgin? Can we ask her for anything? Must we be on our knees? What must we say and how many times? For how much time must we stay? Should we look at her directly? Does it not work if we ask before we thank? Does she work with the faithless and the wavering? Is there a limit to the span of the miracle? Can bodies be transformed? Can a thought be transfixed?

I want to see the pilgrims and go on the saint's day. I want to see the line of faces of people I never imagined existed. See their parasols. See the sale of jovialities and commemoratives and, farther down the line, the sale of neon and misspelled words. Farther, the selling off of lust and elixir. Farther, the sold and the sellouts. The serpentine line of taxis and the lost asking how much does it cost to go anywhere. Approximate. How much does it cost to drop the approximant we?

Should I bring her anything? What do I give to the collection machine? A coin or a bill or a nothing?

An obstruent. I make it only to the gates and ask for miracles through the grates and buy a sweet loaf made with milk rind. I turn towards the heat-bleached vertebrae of the elevated train that enters the city the way a creature slithers through a piece of fruit. Young lady, are you a Catholic? I answer a man, no. Snake through the drunk vendors, and I wouldn't mind being drunk either. Young lady, it's a shame you're not Catholic. A vexing-voice between my shoulders. There, there. Young lady.

Does she need me to believe in this? Does she need me to be a believer? Does she need me?

Soon, a mother will be saved and another too. Soon the tumors will disappear from a sister's lungs and an uncle gets out of prison. Soon, you'll be back here giving her credit. Soon, you're a regular and you don't know even one liar, dying man, faker or cheat. Soon, you'll see.

What do you believe in, honey? Don't know, I answer a man. In nothing.

**

Implosion: the afternoon is high and the sun is direct and the tropics course their meridian and sweet citrus globes loose themselves from their trees and find themselves downhill.

Then, small utterances of pain.

Yes, the susurration of hunger.

Hallelujah, a sustained sonorant.

Thank God, a glottal stop.

II: EXOSKELETON

A PHENOMENALIST'S GUIDE TO THE BLOCK

The block is hot as hell and
Chikungunya is getting things started in the still water on the patio.

I have no sentimentality and leave my wedding shoes out for the taking.
Meanwhile, the printers below run off counterfeit bus tickets.

I get tired of writing how I talk and start writing how I think.
Meanwhile, a water stain starts from God knows where and Everybody knows why.

All the men on the block are paying deposits on glass bottles and having them refilled.
Soon the television comes on and boys with fashion haircuts run a length of green

incessancy. I find I work better while plucking out the bifurcated ends
of my hair. That funny man downstairs is always making the women laugh with jokes
    I can't hear.

Down there, they have radio and coffee and the seesaw of letters:
falsity, falsity, false. Meanwhile, the Religious Supply next door seeks only women aged 18-30

who are presentable and well-mannered enough to sell asceticism. I am out of luck.
A man in the nursing hospital across the way pulls back a blue primeval curtain

making a real disturbance. Meanwhile I, half-naked, rescue plants I've been letting die
on the roof. On the block that's hot as hell. Too much weeping now

for the death of Juan Gabriel. Get a hold of yourselves, good people of Mexico.
    The parade is tired.
An exchange student on her terrace shows a lank boy how to hula with so much sex it's absurd,

absolutely absurd. Meanwhile, a man calculates dough into a thousand airy sheets.
I can only imagine how sweet the vendor on the corner is being, protecting milk from the sun

with his opaque store. Using *usted*. I certainly don't deserve to be talked to with *usted*.
The best disposable products in all the city. The best plastics. The best cakes. Papers. Invites.

Chickens. Bus tickets: falsity, falsity, false. The best, most fresh water poured out just for
    you and yours
into a 20 liter jug and sealed. No airborne, sea-borne, land-borne, insect-borne disease
    possible here.

Meanwhile, two moths circumnavigate the cistern. 75 mosquitos backpedal in the
water of the wash.
The exchange student lets us in on her love. Someone aims for the falsetto of a dead song.

And I am out of luck.

CANTO FOR TWO WOMEN WHO COMMISSIONED A LOVE POEM

Do not do the death march.
Come the government for you.
Come a mutation in your genes.
But do not do the death march.

Do not do the death march
When shaving vanity from your head,
Or hearing, throughout the day,
Your personal call to prayer,

That unresolved interrogation
Of pain that scours the body
And stops, swells, wants.
Your gods cannot be interrogated.

Do not do the death march
When displaced from Jalisco's wilds
To the America of rect sunflowers
And bright machines. Nor should you

Do the death march when in their machines
They mark your blood with contrast
And go illuminating the apexes of events
That are a supposed, projected death.

Do not do the death march when
On the monitor the shape of your lungs
Glows like a body of water irradiated
By the meticulous sight of the full moon.

Nature cannot be interrogated.
There in your lung bodies,
The tubers grow, anamnesis of
The milk of your childhood farm.

Always the idyllic spoils. But never
Do the death march. Come diagnoses,
Come the law, come the rule of the land.
You wouldn't know how to do the death march.

You never have. Nor the good woman beside you.
Neither have ever been ones to march.
Not against the institution nor its cumbersome
hate that suffocates the flame

Of any love that isn't its version:
The candescent love of two women
Hidden so long it starts to burn the chest
That hides it and then metastasizes.

Unhide. Love cannot be interrogated.
Your good woman knows all of your gods,
Calls them by name, invokes the healing
Of all of their hands, and for you. Life, death, even

Their polemics—it's all beautiful—say you.
Beauty cannot be interrogated.
Flash a light into the Styx.
But do not do the death march.

LOOSED SESTINA

Beneath the stutter of the police helicopter,
      muteness, involuted.

Camouflage is
the jagged squares of night.
The gunman in the open side, he's

masked to the eyes, looks us
               down the barrel.

      In the park,
the tree line recoils.
The fountain tulip writhes under the hull.
      Flame of the forest.

The last of the day in sinews.
The man balanced on an axis,
a mother's tether.
               Disjoin.
               Here is

      attentiveness. The walkers wind in
               the evolving dark,

      eyes up towards the muzzle.
      Fatigue is built in a helix.
               Slacken.

      The gun is aimed at
      a lapsed part of me.
               Dismantle.

Load this self into the night
& unfurl its banner.

ENUMERATION AT THE IMMIGRATION OFFICE

13 floors and 1 satellite tower. 3 Colonial-era chandeliers.
Hour in, hour out. Green, digital time. 10:27.
Where do you come from and where are you going?
12 glass stalls: information, processes. 1 list of your rights
as a refugee, 1 as a visitor. 1 bright poster
for the kids being moved. Keep smiling.
1 form letter that says I love and honor.
1 form letter that says I tell the truth.
25 minutes of 2 copies of everything and 3 weeks for 1 decision
on you. 1 you. Is that right?
2 payments. 2 lost receipts equals 6,700 pesos which is
335 dollars, which was 670 dollars once upon a time:
when Mexico had 50 billion more barrels of petroleum,
1 less widespread panic about walls,
1 more rat in the race.
How did we get from there to here?
2 photos of my face (front and profile) in 1 of my 2 palms.
They won't need your photos until they're sure they want you.
2 skinny lawyers on their feet all day.
My 2 expedientes on the 2nd floor labeled
"número único de trámite" (a unique processing number!):
1 file from a former life and 1 from the 1 I live now,
with 6 pictures of my marriage in 6 different locations:
kitchen, ocean, with mother, flash storm, living room, undisclosed.
1 proof of conviviality; 2 fines; 3 ex-visas; 4 white lies. Just like that!
1 more year until permanence. 3 more years until citizenship given
0 detectable errors in my conduct. The official with heavy red
lips has found 3 errors in my solicitude: 1. no apartment number
2. no land line 3. the way I classify my existence is all wrong.
Phantom! no, *¡Ausencia!* yes. 1 computer at which to fix errors.
1 code of 18 characters for my being, 13 for my fiscal obligations to society.
Alphanumerics. Type fast, girl. Type.

Reader:
  tell me.
    What did I set out to tell you?

THE MORNING NEWSPAPER

Imagine a Caravaggio. This is the style: black subtropic night
with a mouth of gray opening to a white scream in the center. Red.
The ochre tongue of a headlight. Three bodies skewed and all sinews,
contorted. The muscling of religious-based guilt. The glutton grounded,
facedown in the dust road of an outskirt, a place with the appearance of
not having "regular" time. Not red but wine in his gashes.
A white T-shirt up around his shoulders. Pixelated depths in his lighted flesh.
One hand on the body, a woman half smiles for the camera,
for the morning newspaper, and the jumpsuited vendors who will peddle
this rendering of tragedy to rush-hour drivers:
stalled, guilted, famished. This woman. She is the focal point, the left of center
star that understands us, here in our cars, and grieves in way that skirts death.
This woman loved this man. She did not love this man. It's all there in
dark and light. Then, in light and dark. An overhead brightness hauls her bare shoulders
into blindwhite, casts her form against the wall of the night. Throws her.
The third figure, gaunt, is collapsed over the body. Why love, we ask. Thinness stark
in a tight tank top. A gaudy, knock-off belt drags at his core. The belt is some kind of
symbolism: doused celebration, the failed talisman of consumerism, sobered
playfulness of brothers. The uncanny-ism of violent ballads: money, whichever vice,
Gucci, Gucci, Prada, Prada, and death. Boy, keep your head down.
Keep the stalkers of the morning news out of your eyes.

Here at the interminate red light we count the ways
we've not died. We remember the one who loves us and doesn't love us all the same.
We recall the law of the land. A fresco. The chiaroscuro of our childhood church.
Guilty, guilty, pleasure, pleasure and the light changes.

AFTER THE ELECTION

All the artists talk of darkness and light.

Mexico mourns and rains unseasonably strange;
in November, an April jacaranda blazes electric.

If only the analogy weren't so easy. The mystics say
karma or dark magic—a matter of the other-worlds,

the Catholics claim God's tears, and the self-involved
sense the forecast is finally sweating their depression.

We get up on the podium and cry climate change
and recite the carbon cycle:

dissolution, absorption, and that you and I are fixed
as are the tiny gasps between us or the painting

of the four horsemen of the apocalypse
or the clothes of the neighbors' baby girl,

who howls all day against the black
vinyls her father plays: Guns N' Roses and sitar

meditations that after hours start to sift
the sediment, even, of my chest, here,

two doors down and alone. On the wrong side of things,
always, it seems. Here, with one slumped houseplant

and another that is doing just alright. Here, with viscid
wine and the exhaust shroud over the living room.

And, all the artists wonder if they are still relevant.

On the news tonight: how to turn a graffitied swastika
into anything else. How to make meaning

from a safety pin. How to make lemons into damned
lemonade. How to make a saccharine drip. I swear:

I cannot turn anything into anything else.
No, the rain is not metaphorical weeping nor is it

locusts or blood or what-have-you—
only elemental and abundant.

The inexplicable the artists seek
is only a plateful of matter.

The secret of the end times
is right there in graphite.

Yet, we artists want to know what will become of us.

I snuff my vain thoughts that lick at the wick.
I put my frivolous body to bed and down-

cast and heavyhearted, I
send a poisonous whisper up.

LA BESTIA

In the pin-drop night the revolution retires into the ground, patched and wrought; in places, untended; in places, a vestige of its former self. The ground is doing its best for us: absorbing the cries of the strays and the churn of the nightshift into its folds so that we hear nothing and we, dumbfounded and muted, might sleep before tomorrow taking on the future with flags and magic markers and fine words. Tonight, you and I and the revolution sleep and the land muffles a history of lamentations and exaltations. The land works on berries and grains. It works on the worm. It buffers our sweet and mild thoughts and those malevolent, too, until we are asleep in the mother country's arms

and, then, the whistle
of *La Bestia* divides the night
in two and *La Bestia* takes off
down the track that splits
the land towards the border like a
line between luck
and probability, entire lives
balanced on top of the train—
the apathetic hand that casts
the dice of elsewhere:

ALEXIS IN TEXAS

The border agent says:
Alexis is a pretty name,
and I know what she wants
to say is that Alexis
is a pretty face, and really,
God-bless-er, because
even deeper beneath
that quip is an apology
for her country
and deeper, a nod
to my husband,
to his three first names
and two surnames,
to his rare and fine
features, to his wry mouth, to
his near-black eyes and near-black hair, like
why, Alexis is a lovely name
like, the son of the root and the
follicle of colonialism,
like a man with his back
against the wall and with
his tender ear to it too—
words warming its soft canal,
Alexis and *Texas;*
she bites her tongue and lets
the rhyme go, stamps his book
and the hounds wrinkle their noses
and lug their slick bodies
on their exacted bones in shame,
and Alexis's heart swells in Texas,
and he calls through a borrowed line
to say: love, do you think they're
flush with embarrassment now?

ENUMERATION ON THE 16 BLOCKS FROM THERE TO HERE

31 dropped coupons for American fast food. 107 very-stubs of cigarettes.
1 chapter of the "humble neurotics anonymous group." *What goes on behind closed doors.*
3 ogee or crenellated arches, saints at their centers. 2 mirrored walls. *But, I don't want to look.*
1 man behind me, shuffling his feet. 1 announcement—wanted: 1 presentable woman.
I might have been, but am not, this presentable woman. Then, 6 black doors identical to mine.
    The discarded
legs of a table, 4. 3 more doors, half-open. *Entre//abiertas,* between openings. Spent plastic flags,
tens of them, the pilgrims having already passed. *Tag: the Virgin was here.*
1 sequinned curtain, 1 zebra-striped love seat. Now, 2 black doors almost like mine
on a variation. Doors too small for humans. 82 styles of tile. Help for the eyes times 2.
    Identical dark
openings. 7 pay phones. *Too fast calls.* 3 masked mouths. 24 assorted canes and walkers for sale
in front of the hospital. A hive of doctors and 1 panicked patron. *Need to make a call?*
    Upside-down
styrofoam meals. Stacked in 1 abandoned window, 4 real cakes, fondant and buttercream:
baptism, first communion, wedding and nondescript sacrament. *Appetite: what is it?*
2 fully open front doors with eyes to their patios. In 1, 4 florals and 12 giant ferns.
    1 bright shrine to the
Virgin. 1 wheelchair, not in use. *This is what it looks like if you open my chest* .
A chart with 24 different prices for 24 different lengths of the 24 hours. In paint:
a man whose lips become a wolf's, a bandaged-faced woman with long white tears.
An abandoned house, an almost abandoned house, the radio on. The radio on in 33 locations.
Finally, a discarded map. Just the one. 1 bill thrown to the wind. *Good for you.* In paint:
a fork on a building for a Mexico without hunger. A sapling, a sapling, another sapling.
2 girls unhappy to identify with their father. 6 different kinds on locks on one door. *No one gets in
or out, I say.* In paint: the honeyed word of God, come see. *But, I don't want to see.* A list of names,
lottery winners. 10 tear off phone numbers for a man who'll lend you cash.
    Everything has a resolution?
1 small white coffin and 15 more for full-grown bodies. Store untended. 1 handwritten sign:
    knock hard.
5 angel-faced urns. *Oh how I've knotted the delicate chain of my life beyond remedy.*
1 funeral and not 1 dry eye. *Must be death unnatural. Tragedy.* About time I get out of my own head.

WILD DECEMBER

Don't look at the window tint, that Medusa on 27-inch chrome stilts, Navigator, gold, adrift like Cristobal Colón—that Medusa with blondish waves and surgical curves. Medusa with a pressed shirt and a full moustache. A Lincoln parks on the corner and an unseen being runs an errand. An unseen being eyes me at the park. Sighs out a "good evening" behind my back. Tails me in traffic, winks at me with an unseen eye. At the shopping center—to the slur of uncanny mirth—an unseen man lifts up his pressed black shirt unveiling a grip—did you see the gun? For how many seconds did you stare?

In the air tonight, the breeze of an enhanced lock of hair, the whispers of a bevy of tongues. A swarm of shadowed eyes. Enough slither to take out a whole state.

Do you know what happens to one who looks through a tinted window? Legend: one's chest becomes a casing. One's baby wants a Dodge Charger. One knows one who knows another who thinks that La Santa Muerte isn't half bad. One's brother shows up to Christmas dinner in elephant-hide boots and leaves the floor black. One's life turns to glass. In the neighborhood, bullets shush under a red shattering of fireworks and people avert their eyes. One becomes anti-observed. One hums the dead hum of a V8 Hemi—

that is what I heard like how I heard that this year
we're going to get a cold snap.

OUT-OF-BODY EXPERIENCE WHILE DRIVING AN UNKNOWN PART OF THE CITY AT NIGHT

Calle Ruiseñor (Mockingbird Street)
It occurs to me that I will see my far-off mother only a countable amount of times more
    in this life.

Calle Pelícano
In order to see my mother, I will have to board a pressurized, metal tube.

Calle Eucalipto
For very little reason and without much warning, flight could cease to exist.

Calle Pino
I will get a stamp in a book every time I see my mother.

Calle Fresno
I've inherited my mother's body.

Calle Ciprés
One must really focus to determine if one is moving or if it's the surrounding system that does.

Calle Cardenal
Who else can see this city?

Calle Halcón (Hawk Street)
This street was never here before.

Calle Rusia
The sky is smug. Not even a moon.

Calle España
My mother depends on currency, Foreign Policy, cardinal direction, and the moon.

Calle Francia
My mother depends on enjambment and caesura.

Avenida Alemania
My mother depends on chiasmus.

Calle Cualquiera
If: in the dark, my mother.
then: I, in the dark.

46

HOLDUP AT THE 7-ELEVEN

I couldn't see the crime at first because the boy vacating the register looked like our cousin—the one who's always in aviator glasses just like the ones on the robber-boy, equally thin, almost equally as baby-faced—No. In the robber-boy's aspect was the handprint of a fresh setback. Him, I couldn't look even right below the rims even though I knew he was reading my silent message: *Go on, boy. Steal. I'm not telling.*

And the boy robbing me might as well have been calling me *miss* and asking for permission to take my money and goods and bag—the keys would be too much—but, *no, son, not today. Thing is I need my cash. And how would I call my mother without a phone?* Wordless bargaining. Weapon in his pants waist like *look, miss, but don't tell, alright(?).* A crack in the voice of his silent message.

Go on, child. Steal. I'm not telling. Take a fistful, a Coke, an aerosol. You're doing this now. All the cash I have to my name heating up but not yet catching fire as I count it in my head. An incoming call at bay deep in my shapeless pocket. Covert data exchanges. A motherboard. Nothing I can give up.

There we were, in an anticlimactic standoff.

The cousin-like one took a last look, a wad of pink gum in his mouth—much different from our cousin's, the mouth—a sharp jaw, smacked-jowl, meanness like the metallic taste that pools up in the mouth after an argument in which someone else tells us who we are. *No, I don't know you at all. Not like our cousin at all.*

There we were, making slack estimations.

A silent message:
when do we decide to hurt each other and when not?

POTABLE WATER ANECDOTE

My husband goes out for water, ours being no good for drinking.
Having earlier fought, I think: go. *Take your time.*
Yet I wait; a minute passes, then two, then a week, a year, a decade.
Still, I am under a weak lamplight, my legs folded over the edge of the bed.
I wait in another room, another nation—it's all the same.
I am still on my bones; the same roughshod body.
My brain's still on the stem—firing up and away and missing.

Like a vision my husband ascends from the street
with a five-gallon jug on his shoulders.
Parched, we serve two glasses and drink to our health.
You'd like to think it's sweet, wouldn't you?
But sweet would be a river.

We lean across the imperfect current of kitchen,
lichen. We look towards each other like we moved towards each other
once across time. He knows it. I know it too:
tenderness is an organism without arms or a head—
it's a fractal that blooms perpetual and out of sight.

THE WALL

You must not write about the wall because the metaphor is dirty.
A fast, insalubrious, coming-right-up metaphor that leaves the body sullen

upon its being written. Try on that sullen body:
    a wall will be built between me and my mother
      un muro se construirá entre mi madre y yo

Now, shake it off.
Never again, never again.

Leave that metaphor out in the sun. Take it down to the corner
with the rest of the things you no longer need.

Better yet, trade it in for a tall ladder. Scale it.
Make some notes from the top.

Jump from its apex. Break your body on the way down.
Write about it all. When you can't run anymore,

write an apology about how far you've come and how
veraciously you've tried. To love mother.

I know you do.
And it's all just *words* anyways.

Until those words are in stone.
And then, you'll know what to do with them.

III: NEGATIVE SPACE

DIRECT ADDRESS

Here is everywhere I've ever been and everywhere I've never been at once.
The one beside me is everyone I've ever known and everyone I've never, too.
The howl from the next apartment is every howl across history and it is also not that.
It is no secret we create reality. The storm settling over the city where I am now is
the storm settling over my past haunts, is the storm at a particular longitude and latitude
on the plane of my thoughts; it is a death wish. Observe the way trees flip
their shamed and pallid leaves up to the sky of the mind, which is just the pre-storm
    color I like.
How terrible will the storm be? How big the wave? It is no secret we create the sea. Swim
with me while there's still time. It is no secret we create each other. I create your golden body
emerging from the 5 o'clock surf of a good day. That's 5 o'clock my time, not yours. I create
the wading of your reality towards my reality and the light I think yours should take when
the sun's in its eyes. You get the idea. It is no secret we create each other. I hear your saying
everything you've ever said and everything you've never said at once. And I don't make
    much of it;
no need to work too hard towards understanding. I have the gilded you and the ghost you
tucked away, exactly where I need them for when I need them. I even have variations.
It is no secret I create what you are to me. And every so often, I observe, really observe, which
is an approximation of forgetting: loosing the mind from its tether and letting the poor
    thing go wild,
letting the mind come to terms with its opposition to the tether, letting it try to obliterate
the tether and run amok amid the laws of nature. Now, because I desire *you*,
I resist calling the mind back in.

CURRENT

A woman cannot die in a foot of water. Nor from little
loves or the womb, from the moon's caprice or the wave:
the oceanic, visual, electric, heard, airborne or the primal.

July of deep rainwater and boys' smirks on the corner,
of the loud flare of the earth's chasm shaking our sleep
awake; is she trying to tell us something?

In July, I write words I don't have inside
in forms I don't know; work comes from a chasm
that closes before I find it.

A woman cannot die from work—that is, from influence
and potential energy, not from the spatial nor the temporal.
But in July, the water wants its way down,

its way back to the root word:
chasma—the hollow—chaos—the void—
the yawn: the word that opens my own mouth.

On July twenty-eighth, at eight-thirty-five p.m., a woman,
caught in a current on the street Hacienda Ciénaga
de Mata—that is, the street called *plantation with*

a wetland ("ciénaga," from the Latin
and nearly homophonous with "blind:"
 "ciega") of marsh plants ("mata,"

from the Latin and nearly
homophonous with "to kill:" "matar")—
dies in a foot of water.

WALK

ambling in the most incapacious callejones of the mind
passageways collapsed throughout the history of temblors
at the fault   the stem of thought   its roots like
leviathan rubber trees tearing up the cement of this
my head city   here the question is what will I say I've done
when it's over   this city overing itself   collapsing window by
collapsing window   I will make nothing good and that's
haphazard as cinderblock   everywhere one hard square
of impatience shifting illegibly under another   if I try to observe now
anything it will be
                          the man there   at 2 o'clock,
his sunward face made lucid   his body under the clarity
of the black-and-white grid of a lap blanket; he's been wheeled out
into the patio to die there   don't make anything of it   it is that simple

MARÍA

I

In the waiting room with María. María once a doctor. María wants
to tell me a secret. Can I help her with her hospital gown? María consumes
a white round self-prescription. Her mind wanders. María wants.
Can I keep a secret? For you, María, I can. María says what
María used to do. María once a doctor. María faded now
before she gets radiated. Can I hold onto her rings? Her gold necklace?
María used to save those who came to her. María once a doctor. Saved lives for free
and all in quiet. María once a savior. I call for the doctor. María's drifting. Save her.

II

In front of the ocean with María. María a savior. María says I better
watch my back. That death growths there; trust her. If the shape of things changes,
she says, I should call her. She'll do it for me: a mini-miracle. María miraculous.
María, your girl. María my girl/our girl/everyone's girl. Here comes the wave. I hear it say:
I know. It already knows how it all goes down. María's got her ear to it.

III

At the mall with María. María so humane. María asks which
handbag should she get, and I know she's dying so I say the loudest one.
The most expensive one. María takes me out for steak and lobster
at a chain restaurant after. María so calm about it all.
Over a chocolate martini, María says: God
doesn't make ugly, not even in death. But. So hard to have faith; I know
I'm bringing her down. María gives me a mantra: may God
forgive me for being a nervous wreck.

LIVE FROM THE U.S.

Over a pirated connection you can get prime time.
Packets, switches, a deal between routers and the Tropicana commercial is your hostage.

Tonight you can hear. You can separate sounds. You can see the synth that plays a tinkling jingle
invoking the utmost security that only reduced-sugar OJ and prime time television can:

what with nuclear missile silos turned luxury shelters in Kansas—complete with red dental chairs,
a shooting range, and images of a goneworld lighting windows that look out onto the lithosphere.

Tonight you think this idea is the grave: goneworld. Say that three times fast. And where
do you end up in your mind? The Tropicana spokesmother switched out now for another,

one with a big backyard, a mosaic patio and a brood of beautiful children from every corner
of the world. And vitamins. You know what you have been known to say:

flowers on the table/a fissure in the family. Tonight, you can separate the spokesmother from
the children, from the lawn, from the dancing array of vitamins and the courtship of health.

Tonight, four-chord tunes don't move you to tears. A clip about better banking doesn't frenzy up
your mind as you x-out the possibility of To Have for To Have Not. But you'll be alright.

A striking fact about the luxury silos: a guard with a semiautomatic weapon keeps their watch.
A miraculous apocalypse survivor? One who doesn't mind not surviving? You know what

you have been known to feel: empathy for the gatekeeper. Special empathy for the doomed.
Extra-special empathy for the wholly self-sacrificing. You know you aren't that good.

The prime time program runs its course. Boys and girls and girls and boys falling in love.
Talking about their future as if it were a smooth marble they warmed in their hands,

that they could toss out and collect again. Something finished and with limited purposes:
entertainment and diversion. Hearing them talk is almost enough. You could almost

forget what you know—more importantly, forget what you think—and gather someone you love
up into in your arms and bore a hole into the mess of everything

(really, everything was the word you wanted there)
and linger a little before the virtual window, unhindered.

THE SWAY

In a public sunken garden,
ferns heady with the scent of rain long left us,
I consider my city and say *see? I do have a heart and see? this is ecstasy*

> : fractured limestone confetti &
> gate guards awaiting quotidian crime
> : lopsided oranges &
> a dead end
> : a doctor's office where imaged organs
> twirl bright through voids
> : this park that shatters in verdancy &
> wrecks its own light

Havoc!
Siren-songs in my earphones.

Mania!
Creatures moving unseen.

> : a felled frond, not dead to me!
> : a discarded list of unwanted things.

Hysteria!
The dogs want nothing to do with me.

I say *see?: my life beyond remedy*
& fidget at the knot in its chain.

MIRROR

From the kitchen, stories:
      how the third child was born the size of the palm of a hand,
      how the first child and the mother (who is speaking) were almost lost
      what, only fourteen was the mother, and too small for so much;
      how the middle child's birth was preceded by the mother's long crawl right up
      to the hem of the basilica's Virgin, and how that child turned out all right from the start:
      a pontificator and sit-straight-upper. A good boy. How on the wound
      you need the cleanest honey you can find. How for the breasts you need
      the sweet liquid yeast, the same for brewing. How you will need
      to seek out thermal waters for healing. How a couple drops
      of essence in brandy will dilate you. How the middle child was birthed
      quick, in transit.
      How big is the wait caused by time.

I hide out in the bathroom observing the strange meditation of lines my body is exerting on
my under eye. I stretch the skin out taut and release. Again.   I swear to God—
if I go out there: *When? For you? A child?* I don't have the heart to descend into the kitchen
where so peaceably yet exuberantly two women converse, without even food or drink before
them, just the sustenance of pure talk coursing their sturdy, loving veins.

That sustenance is what you need to be a believer.

I'll wait for the lull.

LOVE POEM FOR THE PURPORTED END OF THE WORLD

I don't have the heart to tell you
    that this morning

in your absentmindedness
    you left both front doors open

a sight so unholy when I
    hours later   came home to see it

their dangling   the black satin
    sashes of the building

it almost knocked the wind out of me
    in elation   the dust & the flies

could have come for us
    the thief could have

returned for what
    the thief didn't get last time

but why worry you with what
    doesn't need worrying

sometimes no ill enters
    the negative space &

this is how the future
    has always been made

ASH WEDNESDAY

The street is torn up
like the wall of a vacant
home of transgressions.

•

It occurs to me
to sin, steal a red-and-white
squared, trashed sidewalk tile.

•

Black ash in a cross.
The populace's forehead.
Come on. Talk of God.

•

Where the street has gone:
earth. Still alive. Breathing hard.
Its eyes heavenward.

•

I am the odd one
out. Clean forehead like a moon
that nobody needs.

•

Yellow machines sulk.
No one loves you when you're down.
Time to grind the night.

•

Black ash in a cross.
At the market they catch me
weighing right and wrong.

•

Tomorrow the street
will be new. The smooth ore of
confession. Tell me.

•

It crosses my mind
to sin, take a red-and-white
lie out for a walk.

•

Tomorrow, reform.
Tomorrow, today. I want
to help you, I do.

*

Black ash in a cross.
A man eyes me down across
a bounty of fruit.

•

The street, *Reforma*,
gets reformed. See how easy?
Now you. Now me too.

DISSONANCE

My mother laughs a hysterical laugh about death
across the invisible cord between us. She is making death sound like
something one makes in the kitchen: bread fashioned by hand. She laughs
and wipes the work of laughing off as if on an apron.

My mother will not stop laughing, even when the call is cut
and silence surrounds me on my end of the world;
silence: a universe as intricate and wrought as any.

And I'm gone in it. Gulped up. Bargaining.

TRUE

There are things that are true
    that are at the same time false. I made them

false. Laments: I throw them back
    into the chaos (there, they can become

what they like). Unpaid bills. Muddied prints.
    Diatribes in 4/4 time or verse.

Other truefalse things I stuff under the rug
    or drown in the oil-slick heart of an other.

One truefalsehood is that I lost a woman
    in the metro. Another is that I simply

let friends go. That I don't have a hand in
    relegating unwant to the crawl space.

Even more obscured: things like that night
    I made a stranger drive me out to the island.

I could tell you now that all around were
    pious stars and that the sea was

the sea and minding its own, or
    that I was only a sister in need, but

I could only tell you that now
    because depending on the day

I drop my life into water or
    cover it with a thick slab of muck

and believe in the result:
    however it looks on whichever day.

Thus, I've lost: yellow afternoons
    and the pattern on the curtains,

the visage of the stray, the current
	of my husband's hair, the rules

of night, the science of shadows,
	my shadow, the timbre of voices.

From time to time, someone will stun
	me and ask for identification. Awe at it, I do—

Name: true. Eyes: true. Home: true.
	Good down to the digits. I wait for them

to tremble and morph, a 2 to become a 3. Then,
	I could shake my head and wring my hands,

(so hard I've worked on fallacy, I could cry)
	Yes. I could cry from my frenetic void:

now, when they need to,
	how will they identify me?

APOLOGY

Sometimes I forget where I am.

I go as far as the patio and hear
three dogs wailing into the night.
Dogs that still have ardor in them. I see
shadows that fold into the honey of dirt
and its fruits being molded into shapes.
The silver tooth of some sister somewhere.
Someone, somewhere, not dying.

A town on the horizon lights
the neon disquiet of its church's cross.
A junction of blood and passion,
ardor and damnation. Someone waits
for the cows to come home. They do.
Some sister reclines content,
the food gone cold. Content like we do.

I mean this: I could taste the tongues
of the agave pointing up through the earth.
I could feel the spines
of renegade paperbacks
folding in every deranged corner
from here to *el D.F.* I saw ardor.
I could touch ardor. I could know that it
was what made the plaster separate
from the patio wall and what made
the brick beneath into that strong cage.

And then I had an idea. A dark fantasy:
a couple argues over nothing just before a great quake.
They retreat into their corners:
one on the patio, the other in bed.
The bedroom collapses. The patio survives.
Over nothing.
Can you believe it? Over nothing.

I swear this: I could feel my hand burned
by the interior of the bell hot
with so many sung songs. I could see Jupiter.

The beacon of a vessel. The North Star.
I could hear a memorial march, a siren,
a tinkling game, and the growing of
the neighbors' baby's bones.

I went to you. My country a disaster.
The house held up by ardor.

ARTICULATION

A Michoacán pine loosens a spirant into the night, and deeper, the collective forest modulates a fricative. Deeper yet, the forest on fire. Silently. Suddenly: I hate everything I've ever written. Even the alright utterance. The forest, on the other hand, really knows how to put an observation between its teeth and let it speak for itself: order in not disrupting the order.

•

In June, advances. The rain. The frog mates. The velvet spider emerges. June: the whip snake, the reproduction of the winged ant. Owl song at night. Long-legged mosquitos abound. The mantle of the Virgin effloresces. Plovers roam the riverbank. Aphrodisiacs give. The cork tree flowers against extinction. June: germination. June: cinders.

In July, abundance: insectalia, snails, the wood mushroom, grand mushroom, wild, Amanita Caesarea, Agrocybes. The perfumed flowers of Saint John. The temporal stream. July: the serpent is born. Doves eat. Sulfur butterflies land on clover. The praying mantis camouflages in a goldfinch song. The Pingüicola remains a carnivorous plant, mouth open. Fawn.

In August, proliferation. The Immortelle Sempervivum, everlasting flower. Guava. Dung beetles in their nest. The ground flush with Amanita Alexander. For one day or two, the adult Ephemera lives. August multiplies: the pendicule of agave, vertices on anise. Cronartium fungus blights the pine. The grand design of the dogface butterfly. The wild dove cuts air. Come eat the forest floor.

In September, inflorescence. Dahlia. Horsetail. Moss. The marigold, sweet-scented. September: the fire ant eats. Croaking goes on. As does collecting. The rat's on the prowl. Plants root in the air. Stars grow in the ground.

In October, flight. The voracious dragonfly hunts. Lepidoptera: zebra, Eurema Mexicana, Nathalis Iole in the river channel. The red-winged woodpecker is observed. The skunk rules the superfamily. Buzzards on the cleanup. The quick glitch of the Phoebis Philea. In October, an entire cosmos grows from the ground. An extinct species is missed.

In November, last waters. The puma takes and the coati gives. The fox takes and the red-tailed hawk lances. November emergence: the velvet wasp, bats. Cooly, the Vinegaroon quiets under the rock. Briefly, the river crab shows. In the gully, the green vine snake. The puma is taken. The puma is missed. Birds fly at half-mast.

In December, suspension. Only abundance is in the gullies. The moon flies on the back of the moth. Lichens quit. Deer give in to a new color. The grass sullies itself in fruit. Winter enters. December of the sleeping serpent, and in the lowest places, the white-collared seedeater.

In January, rings. Morning of the deer-eyed moth. The stick insect, Phasmatodea, rounds in the leaves, a ghost. The motmot swings its pendulum tail. The whip snake gyres for food. The mind of the spider circles. The mind of the weasel paces in wait. Industrious January: the rattlepod, paper wasp, solitary eagle and white-tail. The virulent Aphididae makes haste under the leaves. The Michoacán pine throws seed.

In February, sanctuary: fauna takes shelter and mantinal vapors rise from the thermal river. Leptophobia enters flowers. They hang their heads before the nature shrink. In February, jeopardy: beneath the rocks, the mother scorpion; the Vermillion Flycatcher all dextrous; the armadillo and the river turtle turned callous. Wait. Wait. Wait for food. Without leaves, the Ceiba waits for cover. Time for the February fox-romp, Fiscal-Shrike-hang, coyote-call. The coyote wants a partner in crime. The black widow suspends her eggs. The chokecherry is full.

In March, risk, but: turtledoves court and the Oleander Hawk moth reposes on the oak. The Jerusalem cricket, a baby-faced villain, discovers pain. The alder discovers its flowers. The Groove-billed Ani screeches. In March: denticulate leather bugs and the roadrunner. Very agile, that black swallowtail. Heated, that Calandra Lark. Beguiling, that dragonfly nymph. Spurious, that son-of-a-gun fake coral snake: Scarlet King.

In April, vacuousness. Nobody light a match. The serpent, dizzy-deluded, sheds its skin and takes cover, poor soul. Between thorns, the cactus flower emerges. The Pine disseminates a tract and the Copperwood makes a paper storm, raving for its lost leaves. The insipid ficus of the cloud forest spins its head. The virulent Aphididae is circumlocuted by the sweet-tongued ladybug. Feminism takes hold on the pine, conical. Swallows, swallows, more swallows.

In May, extremity: Kingfisher, adult dragonfly, fish in the hot current. Irregular flight. Love in the thicket. Grackle in the sentry. The scorpion abounds and gall grows. The Clouded Yellow gets high on libating nectar. Serpents reproduce. The cryptic Cracker is often confused for tree bark. Deer shed their antlers on the cottonmouth floor. No one even look at a match. Even the tarantula fights for life.

Strike a surface with a matchstick and another short short year goes up in flames.

•

You and I won't be able to do that—what with the high vowels we bemoan. Beneath them: *need to know, need to know.* You and I won't be able to do what the forest right outside of us does. Out there it happens like this: in one breath, the shrike hangs its prey. In another, the forest mourns even the absence of the turkey. And not a word about it. Not the least extrapolation.

If I'm ever able to write, it will sound like that.

If I'm ever able to write, it will be a pine spirant or collective fricative. It will be a forest fire and a neck-snap. A skin shed, and another another another